Li

with the...

NEXT
BIG
THING

Charlie Mills

Living

with the...

NEXT
BIG
THING

Charlie Mills

NEW HOLLAND

To my eternally patient parents

This edition first published in 2008 by New Holland Publishers (UK) Ltd
London • Cape Town • Sydney • Auckland
www.newhollandpublishers.com
10 9 8 7 6 5 4 3 2 1

Garfield House, 86–88 Edgware Road, London, W2 2EA, United Kingdom
80 McKenzie Street, Cape Town, 8001, South Africa
Unit 1, 66 Gibbes Street, Chatswood, NSW 2067, Australia
218 Lake Road, Northcote, Auckland, New Zealand

ISBN 978 1 84773 276 7

Senior Editor: Kate Parker
Editorial Direction: Rosemary Wilkinson
Illustrations: Tom Hughes
Cover design: Zoe Mellors and Tom Hughes
Design: Zoe Mellors
Production: Melanie Dowland

Photographs (t=top, b=bottom, l=left, c=centre, r=right): page 44: tl © Araldo
di Crollalanza/Rex Features; tc © iStock/Craig McKay; tr © Kristin Callahan/
Rex Features; bl © Ray Tang/Rex Features; bc © iStock/Payam Hanzei;
br © James Curley/Rex Features; page 45: tc © Michael Simon/Rex
Features; tr © iStock/Julie Masson; bl © James Curley/Rex Features;
bc © iStock/RTimages; br © ITV/Rex Features

Reproduction by Pica Digital PTE Ltd, Singapore
Printed and bound in Malaysia by Times Offset (M) Sdn Bhd

CONTENTS

LADIES AND GENTLEMEN, INTRODUCING.... THE

Next!
Big!
Thing!

What are celebrities really like before they become famous?

You might know already, if you are living with the

Next Big Thing

   Right now you might think some of her behaviour – like an obsessive interest in fashion, TV and fully-fledged celebrities – is a bit peculiar. You look on in disbelief as she tries to fit the scrabbling family dog into her handbag like a suburban tribute to Paris Hilton. And why does she insist you roll out a red carpet on the driveway every afternoon when she comes home from school? Is she mad? Fret not. These formative years are important: she is like young Mozart immersing himself in the whole concerto of fame, soaking up the secrets of her trade in order to become its queen. All those nights spent watching 'X Factor' and dressing up for no apparent reason will not be in vain.

True, it is baffling how a mini-person can know (or indeed care) so much about hemlines and hairspray, and be able to discuss at length the difference between one pair of jeans and another, which (to the untrained eye) are virtually identical. The Next Big Thing is as sensitive to changes in fashion as a polar bear is to global warming. Without a carefully controlled image, the Next Big Thing may as well set up camp on a rapidly shrinking iceberg herself.

If you have blind faith in the unwavering confidence of the Next Big Thing, the advent of superstardom is nigh. Fame is a fast-paced world so it can prove a little bewildering to even the most grounded parent. As one who is living with the Next Big Thing, the best advice you can have is 'go with it', but that is as supportive as a push off a cliff. Fortunately, this book is here to take your hand, guide you through the darkness and propel you towards the spotlight.

You will learn to understand what motivates your Next Big Thing, how to encourage and cajole her, and how to make sense of her many moods. Most importantly, you will arm her with the skills to negotiate everyday life and inspire her to be as together as you.

In years to come, you may even become famous yourself off the back of your young star. Take up the reins where Britney Spears' mother Lynne got thrown off and sell stories to the red-tops about the time your Next Big Thing danced a hole in your living room carpet or sold your collection of antique tea chests to pay for a sequinned minidress. Ah, what misty-eyed memories. This is a time to treasure, not to check into The Priory yourself. *Living With The Next Big Thing* will help you do just that.

HOW TO SPOT THE
Next Big Thing

To a novice like yourself, Next Big Thing's behaviour pushes the boundaries of 'normal'. Recognise any of these?

		YES	NO
1	Does she refer to her bedroom as the VIP area?	☐	☐
2	Has she adjusted the lighting in the kitchen so a spotlight casts flattering shadows on her face?	☐	☐
3	Look at a recent collection of family photos. Is she posing at the front and centre of every frame?	☐	☐
4	Despite having no cash, does she seem determined to buy expensive things an ordinary person couldn't afford without at least 10 years of wages under her professional belt?	☐	☐
5	Has she asked more than three times to have her ears pierced?	☐	☐

	YES	NO

6   Does she see it as her duty to give you a little nudge about your appearance when you are not looking as presentable as she would like? ☐ ☐

7   Has her teacher told her why her role in the school play is actually the most important one, despite it involving only seven lines? ☐ ☐

8   If your house was burning down, do you worry she would be too busy watching TV to notice? ☐ ☐

9   Is your Sky+ so hard at work recording fame-hungry talent programmes that the machine has a right to demand a percentage of your little star's future earnings? ☐ ☐

10   Is she in possession of the belief that your credit card is actually hers, to do with what she likes? ☐ ☐

If you answered YES to five or more of these, then congratulations! You are living with the Next Big Thing.

BEING THE NEXT BIG THING:
The Rules

RULE 1

If you must purchase a designer knock-off from the market, do make sure you have a suitable disguise to hand. Dark glasses are a girl's best friend, but a fake moustache and big plastic nose combo will be your soulmate.

RULE 2

Why stand around slack-jawed when you can pout?

RULE 3

If a family member requests the honour of having you for a bridesmaid, do your best not to upstage the bride. However, if she looks a little clumsy during the first dance, help out by stepping in and recreating the *Dirty Dancing* lift with the groom.

RULE 4

It is worth practising your Kylie tribute at home before giving it to Simon Cowell with both barrels.

RULE 5

Whenever you are in a troublesome dilemma, ask yourself, what would *High School Musical*'s Gabriella Montez do? The answer is always: go out with the cute basketball team captain, wear snazzy clothes and get noticed for your, um, amazing singing.

RULE 6

Do not be a slave to the mirror. Shop windows, CCTV monitors, car bonnets and puddles are all useful reflective surfaces.

RULE 7

Fake tan is the orange badge by which you recognise your own kind. Sure, you might look a *little* tango-tastic right now, but if the paparazzi jump out from behind that bush you will have a lovely golden tan in the resulting pictures. That's what really matters.

RULE 8

Book your diary up weeks in advance with ballet practice, vocal rehearsals and shopping marathons to make yourself feel busy and important. It also prevents you from partaking in rounds of pesky chores that parents like to throw in your spokes. Your delicate hands will never unload the dishwasher again.

RULE 9

If someone asks, 'WHAT are you WEARING young lady?' take a moment to sit down and talk them through how you put your outfit together. Not everyone has your fabulous sense of style, bless 'em.

RULE 10

Should you run out of money, have a word with the Bank Of Mum And Dad. Suckers.

EVOLUTION OF A STAR

Was your little girl adopted by fame-hungry aliens, or is there another explanation for how the Next Big Thing came into being?

Move along folks, there's
nothing to see here. She is
just a normal teenager,
innocently climbing trees and
happily skimming stones,
wearing a pair of ill-fitting
hand-me-down jeans. But
gradually, she spends the
summer months inside
watching 'Big Brother' instead
of cartwheeling on the lawn.
'I'm A Celebrity Get Me Out
Of Here' follows, and
Christmas fades into the
background as 'X Factor' and
'Strictly Come Dancing' battle
for her attention. The energy
she used to burn off running
around outside is now
simmering within her, waiting
for its moment to leap out.
Then she utters the five
words that strike seismic
fear into the heart of your
being: 'I want to be
famous.'

STAGE 2

You are late for work because she takes so long to get ready in the morning. She has always enjoyed singing in the shower, but now everything she does is a performance. The tiled kitchen floor is perfect for tap dancing, evidently, and she finds it hard to sit through a meal without breaking into Lionel Blair's most celebrated moves. No longer is she content to wear her older brother's cast-offs. For the first time, she breaks open her piggy bank and takes an interest in shopping. You have noticed she has adopted a limping walk that is probably down to her new high heels, her first pair. Bravely, she smiles through the blisters. She has transformed her bog-standard pay-as-you-go mobile phone into a fashion item with the help of diamante stickers. Her room looks like where old *OK!* magazines go to die.

Now her piggy bank is
but an empty carcass,
she has convinced you to
pay for singing and dance
lessons after school. She is
dedicated and disciplined and
you cannot help but admire her
newfound sense of purpose –
if only she did not wear clothes
appropriate for a cabaret bar
for a trip to Sainsbury's. When
everyone in the produce aisle
stares, she faux-blushes from
behind a stack of
bananas then
shimmies off to inspect
the shelves bursting with
magazines. She does not seem
to require an audience; even at
home she has special outfits for
lounging around on the sofa:
legwarmers, sweatbands and a
sparkly leotard, like an off-duty
kid from *Fame.* When you wear
those clompy shoes, she refuses
to acknowledge you in public.
This is only a phase, right?

Wrong. Whole weekends have been given over to the mighty stage school / shopping combo. She has boarded a runaway train, presumably paying for the ticket with your exhausted credit card. You try to reason with her: 'Do you really need another pink top when you have two already?' She defeats you with a heavenwards roll of the eyeballs and begins redecorating her bedroom to cope with her ever-expanding wardrobe. Despite having no money of her own to put in it, she insists on swinging a (new, different) ladylike handbag by her side whenever you leave the house. She is experimenting with make-up and if you catch her at the wrong angle she looks uncannily like Lily Savage. If you hear her begging to have her ears pierced one more time you might just get a staple gun and do it yourself.

'Get me an agent!' she cries. Is it your imagination or has she developed an American accent? She keeps threatening to become famous and giving you advice on how to look a little less shabby. She dresses up for the flimsiest of occasions, like wearing a little cocktail dress even when chatting to her friends *online*.

Does she even know what a cocktail tastes like? You hope not. You feel a wee bit envious of how glamorous her life has become as you chauffeur her to another party, dance or shopping date, still wearing your pyjamas. The pressure of her impossibly grand expectations is becoming too much for you to bear.

She looks happy though, bless her, and that is what you try to focus on when a reporter from *The Sun* comes by to ask what it is like living with the Next Big Thing.

LIVING WITH THE NEXT BIG THING:
DOs and DON'Ts

DOs

1 DO be warned that the Next Big Thing is every advertiser's dream. She is a sucker for every product going, be it a hair-braiding kit, home karaoke set or glitter-wheeled rollerblades. She must have them all, as a matter of urgency.

2 DO try to teach Next Big Thing the difference between 'want' and 'need'. As in, 'I don't NEED another pair of new shoes until the soles are worn right through,' and not, 'I want another pair of sparkly heels so I can forget about them by next month and drive my parents crazy when I scream that I have nothing to wear.' It is worth a shot.

3 DO write a nice letter to Gordon Brown, cc-ing the Inland Revenue, explaining that your family deserves a tax break because the Next Big Thing is single-handedly keeping the economy from dying on its ass.

4   DO make her happy by pretending you thought her singing was actually a song on the radio. If that doesn't bag you a generous birthday present, nothing will.

5   DO point out her pimples, particularly if she tries to cover them with make-up. Remind her spots are a sign she is growing up, thus she should wear each one like a pus-filled badge of pride.

6   DO ask her when, 'Mwah! Mwah!' became acceptable in common parlance. It hasn't? Well then, please stop that ridiculous air-kissing routine.

7   DO remind her that, in Britain, 'cheerleader' is not a legitimate job description or ambition.

8   DO avoid asking Next Big Thing for input when you redecorate the living room, or you will end up turning it into a pink sparkly Santa's grotto.

9   DO say, 'I bet you can't make emptying the bins look glamorous,' because she just might do it and save you a dirty job.

10   DO join her when she bursts into song. It is the fastest way to shut her up.

DON'Ts

1   DON'T be afraid to use the magic words, 'No, we can't afford it,' as many as 200 times a day. At some point in the distant future, the message will sink in.

2   DON'T think, even for the mini-est of moments, that once you buy her that denim skirt she won't 'need' any more clothes until next year.

3   DON'T be surprised when you overhear her entertaining her friends by royally taking the Michael out of you.

4   DON'T ask her to help you find an outfit for your cousin's wedding, unless of course you have two weeks to spare and are happy to buy something for her in every shop.

5   DON'T presume she is too young to understand the concept of a phone bill. The proverb may say, 'The best things in life are free' but that does not include ear-meltingly long telephone sessions. The sooner she gets her head around that, the better.

6   DON'T be offended when she rejects the perfectly nice name you chose for her and elects to call herself 'Stardust', 'P Giddy', 'Miss Terious' or some similarly ill-advised moniker.

7   DON'T launch a full-scale personality assault on Next Big Thing's ex-best-friend, even if she is sly, precocious and smells slightly of cat litter. The pair of them are sure to make up next week and Next Big Thing will innocently repeat your prize comments word for word.

8   DON'T let her see how much you need that glass of Merlot when the clock strikes seven, or your authority will be forever compromised.

9   DON'T let Next Big Thing name the family dog because you will be the one shouting, 'Here, Pinky Pookums,' in the park.

10 DON'T put it past her to raise cash for a new dress by eBaying 'some old crap' she found in the loft. Take this moment to remind her that (a) 'crap' is a subjective description, and (b) that would be **your** old crap, then. (Not any more though – some lucky bidder has won it at auction for 17 pence.)

Welcome inside the most exclusive club in Britain: Next Big Thing's bedroom. This is where stardust is sprinkled over her suburban existence, making her become absolutely fabulous. Here is what you can expect to find:

1   Dressing table. **Covered in lip glosses, lip liners,
lipsticks, lipsalves, lip-plumpers, eyeliners, eyeshadows,
eyelash curlers, eye pencils, eyebrow-shaping kits and
further variations on this theme. How can one small face
possibly be home to all of these products?**

2   Posters **of Zac Efron, David Beckham, Captain Jack
Sparrow and some boy from 'Hollyoaks'. Ponder on this:
When (not 'if', please, have a little faith) the Next Big
Thing marries one of these handsome young fellows in
years to come, she will be able to bashfully tell the
newspapers, 'When I was little I had his poster on my
bedroom wall.' At this point, please refrain from
mentioning that there were other boys in the running, or
you may not get to sit in the front row at the wedding.**

3   Walk-in wardrobe. **Much like the Tardis, the Next
Big Thing can be lost in here for days at a time. It might
look like there has been an explosion in here, but in fact
there is a system to the chaos and if you touch anything
you will be in very serious trouble.**

4   Computer. **'Ah,' you think, with some pride, 'The Next
Big Thing is applying herself to her schoolwork and may
turn out to be a Nobel Prize-winning geneticist after all.'
Stop. You are kidding yourself. That computer is only there
because it has a special programme that matches outfits
together and makes a note of when she last wore that
skirt so she is never caught in the same ensemble twice.**

5   Mirrors. **Never a moment goes by without her being
able to monitor the fluttering of her eyelashes or inspect
a panoramic view of her new shoes.**

6   Framed photographs. **Aah, the Next Big Thing looks so fabulous in all of these photos. Funny, that. When you check the memory card on your camera, you will notice she has deleted every unflattering shot of herself so it looks like you are the only gurner in the family.**

7   Unidentified junk. **For someone who never fails to look anything less than polished, it is a mystery how her bedroom contains so much rubbish. Piles of beads, sparkly scarves, handbags, magazines, notes, shoes, discarded toys and lord-knows-what-else cover every surface.**

8   Dream factory. **The Next Big Thing's mini four-poster bed is fit for a princess. Draped with chiffon and covered with big marshmallow-y pillows, her bed is the place where she retires at night, confident that another hurdle on her march to the top has been turned to dust. When she wakes every morning, her dream of being dazzlingly famous burns ever brighter within her.**

9   Toys. **As well as an old Malibu Barbie, piles of rainbow-coloured teddy bears and a lollipop-headed Bratz, you are relieved to find the scraggy old blanket she carried around throughout her toddling years. Though it is grey now and smells a wee bit fruity, you clutch it to your cheek at the memory of your little girl's long-lost innocence of the world of merchandise.**

10 Top secret diary. **'Read me!' it whispers, determined to seduce you. 'Read me and ye shall know the innermost workings of the Next Big Thing's mind.' Oh, but it is tempting. V-e-r-y tempting. Can you really wait until she turns 18 and publishes it as a bestselling autobiography?**

WHAT NOT TO SAY
To the Next Big Thing!

Living in the same house as the Next Big Thing, someone pre-ordained for higher things, can be challenging for a civilian (i.e. non-celebrity) like you. It is difficult to know what to say to make her happy. Be careful not to let these diamond phrases trip off your tongue:

'Oooh, I like your watch. Did you buy it with Esso tokens?'

'Honestly, this cycle helmet will make your hair look hot.'

'HEY GIRLFRIEND, LET'S HANG OUT IN THE LIBRARY ON SATURDAY NIGHT.'

'Have you considered dying your hair pink to match your nails, shoes, dress, coat and handbag?'

'Why is your skin so orange?'

'Isn't that your boyfriend in *The Sun* with his arms around another girl?'

'I think we should get rid of the TV and spend our evenings reading improving novels. Yeah?'

'WHAT DO YOU THINK ZAC EFRON LOOKS LIKE WITHOUT MAKE-UP?'

'I've decided to audition for 'X Factor' myself. Shame you're not old enough.'

'What do you mean? Why can't I wear these boots with these jeans!'

'Do you really think I need plastic surgery?'

'I don't think your school skirt is quite short enough.'

'Justin Timberlake called, but I can't find the bit of paper I wrote his number on.'

'You don't mind if I tag along to the cinema with you and your boyfriend, right?'

'PLEASE CAN YOU PASS ME THE REMOTE CONTROL?'

'I got an email from my friend Steven Spielberg asking if I knew any young actresses he should cast in his new film, but I couldn't think of anyone.'

LET MUSIC BE YOUR GUIDE

A song for every occasion!

The Next Big Thing is so immersed in pop music it is hard to get her to listen to what you have to say.

Fortunately, the record doctor is here to help – dotted throughout this book you'll find helpful suggestions for lyrics to quote in specific situations. Or, if you cannot find an appropriate lyric for your situation, simply say what needs saying and then claim you heard Lily Allen say it recently on TV. No one messes with her.

When Next Big Thing hysterically points out that you have shrunk her favourite top in the washing machine and it is now ruined – 'Ruined! Ruined! I hate you!' etc. – insert your earplugs and sing this little conscience-cleaner:

'Nobody's perfect!
I gotta work it!
I know in time I'll find a way
Nobody's perfect.
Ya live and ya learn it!
'Cause everybody makes mistakes
Nobody's perfect!
Nobody's perfect! No no! Nobody's perfect!'

Hannah Montana: 'Nobody's Perfect'

Is Next Big Thing a little moody when her alarm clock rings in the morning? Give her get-up-and-go routine a little more sha-boom with these rousing lines:

*'I can hear the bells,
My head is spinning.
I can hear the bells,
Something's beginning'*

Hairspray: 'I Can Hear The Bells'

When Next Big Thing was knee high to a chart-topper, she believed that YOU were the coolest person on the planet. Want to rekindle that warm, fuzzy glow within her?

*'There can be miracles, when you believe
Though hope is frail, it's hard to kill
Who knows what miracles you can achieve
When you believe
Somehow you will...
You will when you believe'*

Leon Jackson: 'When You Believe'

When the family would appreciate the Next Big Thing's help in clearing up after dinner:

*'Together, together, together everyone
Together, together, come on let's have some fun
Together, we're there for each other every time
Together, together come on let's do this right'*

High School Musical: 'We're All In This Together'

If you believe it is high time Next Big Thing turned off the TV and did some homework, try this:

*'Something kinda ooooh,
Makes my heart go boom boom
Something 'side of me,
Wanting what you do-oooh'* (your homework now or you're grounded, missy)

Girls Aloud: 'Something Kinda Ooooh'

STAR STYLE AND GROOMING

Cleanliness may be next to godliness, but grooming yourself to within an inch of your life is even better.

Beauty is skin-deep, thus if you apply several layers of make-up over the top, you will be even more beautiful. And deep, too. Right?

As the Next Big Thing, the pressure to look like herself, only a zillion times better, is all-consuming. Here's how she puts the look together...

HIGHLIGHTS

HAIR
EXTENSIONS

SUPERSIZE
SUNNIES

GIRLY HAIR
ACCESSORIES

EARRINGS

FAKE TAN

COAT

T-SHIRT

HANDBAG

ACRYLIC
NAILS

HIGH
HEELS

MINISKIRT

Fake tan. **An absolute must. Without it, people will see the normal shade of her skin and realise she is a living, breathing human being and not a plastic-faced Barbie after all. That would just be too, too awful. So, she applies fake tan as if there is no tomorrow and wears her dirty orange palms like stigmata.**

Acrylic nails. **You could interpret the wearing of fake nails as an attempt to get back to a simpler, more animalistic life, where humans used their claws to protect their family and survive in the wild. Or, you could shake your head and slump to the ground, weeping, sobbing and rocking as you realise the vice-like grip WAGs have on the world. As your tears dry, you get a moment of clarity: the Next Big Thing is only wearing acrylic nails so she can claim scrubbing dried pesto off saucepans is impossible. Canny lass.**

Hair extensions. **Because you have cruelly forbidden her to get mega-expensive hair extensions, she has been to Claire's Accessories and purchased a clip-on ponytail in cheapest nylon. It looks even worse than it sounds. Her whole head crackles with static electricity and bad taste.**

Highlights. **At the salon, Next Big Thing selects her hair colour of choice: honey blonde, silver blonde, gold blonde, this-is-my-natural-colour-honest blonde, star blonde, superstar blonde, banana blonde and this-is-all-my-mum-will-pay-for blonde. Sounds unnerving, but the more dangerous option is forbidding her to go to the hairdresser's; she'll only bleach a**

hole in your best towels doing a DIY job in the bathroom.
Better go upstairs and check she's not in there right now.

Earrings. If Next Big Thing breaks a nail she will cry out in
pain, yet she welcomes the agony of having her ears pierced.
Until the day you give her the big OK, she is resigned to stick-
on earrings that stick everywhere else but her earlobes, and
dangly clip-ons that drag her earlobes down so low you
confuse her for an elephant.

High heels. Shoes are made for walking. Next Big Thing
seems to have lost sight of that, as she limps along in her high
heels. The only thing that could possibly make her take notice
of her foot health is a new TV show, provisionally entitled
'Britain's Got Talented Chiropodists', where chiropodists correct
young feet savaged by ill-fitting shoes and then send their
young wards onto the stage to show off their fancy footwork.
Write to ITV about it now.

Miniskirt. In school, teachers carry a tape measure to
monitor skirt lengths in official uniform checks. Maybe you
should employ the same tactic at home!

Coat with no warming properties whatsoever.
Argh, the curse of the 'fashion coat'… it is neither waterproof
nor sufficiently insulating to prevent Next Big Thing from
getting pneumonia in April. Do not let her leave the house
without a thermal vest.

Handbag. **When the family dog is not whimpering to be set free from it, Next Big Thing's handbag is jammed with a collection of lip glosses, hairbrushes and love letters. In a few months, she will be 'like, totally _over_' this bag and onto another one. You can have a good nose in it then.**

Girly hair accessories. **How is it that her small head has space for so many hairbands and clips? Next Big Thing's daisy-studded hairstyle deserves a spot at the Chelsea Flower Show.**

Supersize sunnies. **It can't be convenient for Next Big Thing's sunglasses' lenses to grow larger than ping-pong bats. Spare her the stress of shopping for next season and buy her a welder's visor to cover her whole face. Very _Flashdance_.**

T-shirt with inappropriate slogan. **Does she even know what, 'My other ride is your dad' means? Be afraid. Be very afraid.**

WARNING!

Celeb-Endorsed Tat

A special note on celebrity-endorsed products: there is nothing a savvy star won't do to squeeze another buck out of your Next Big Thing. It's up to you to help her resist.

THE FOUR
GREAT FAME TRAPS

When a young girl embarks on the road to fame and glory, she is vulnerable to falling into a few potholes along the way.

With this guide, you can help ease her path...

TRAP #1:
Not realising less is more

Just like Jordan, the Next Big Thing is prone to doing things she thinks will only make herself look better, which in fact only make her look worse. Wearing clothes of the wrong size, for example. Using such a heavy combination of foundation and fake tan her face is practically paralysed, for another. There is more. Most pressingly: trying to walk in heels so toweringly painful they make _your_ eyes bleed, never mind the injury done to her feet; and styling her hair so much that she would actually look better bald. The list goes on, but you get the idea. She needs saving from herself.

What's the magic answer?

Take her to Clarks to be fitted with the widest, most sensible pair of shoes money can buy, then attach a bulky oven glove to each hand with duct tape so she is prevented from fiddling with her appearance any more.

TRAP #2:
Behaving as if she has an expense account

Well, she kinda does: it's you. The only other person in Britain who does not carry cash is The Queen and that is because she is in the habit of being given things everywhere she goes. Unfortunately the Next Big Thing does not share HRH's good fortune. Take time to teach her how to manage her own money and you save her from a lifetime of bankruptcy, bulldog-faced debt-collectors and the

indescribable hell of living out an 'EastEnders' storyline from the wrong side of the screen.

What's the magic answer?

Keep asking to borrow cash off her until she gets a kick out of stashing her pocket money under her mattress and never spending a penny of it, lest you try to spend it for her.

TRAP #3:
Falling in love faster than Lewis Hamilton wins Grand Prix

Not an hour goes by without Next Big Thing practically levitating with the effort of telling you how much she loves, *loves, LOVES* her new hairband / Leon Jackson / 'Hollyoaks' / delete as appropriate. You are worried about her blood pressure. And what if she runs out of love in later life, when you are old and decrepit and more in need of her affections than ever?

What's the magic answer?

Every time she uses the L-word, remind her no one will ever love her like you do. That won't make for dysfunctional relationships in the future. Not at all.

TRAP #4:
Burnout

If a typical day involves school, singing practice, shopping, dance rehearsals, fiddling with hair, lengthy phone conversations, trying on clothes, the watching of at least one all-singing-all-dancing DVD and a late night session earnestly chatting to her friends online – plus all the effort it takes to wheedle her wicked way with you and not forgetting the shrieking, skipping, giggling and whooping (breathe, breathe) that accompanies Next Big Thing's every move, is it surprising so many child stars burn out young?

What's the magic answer?

Move the family to Pennsylvania, USA, and become Amish. There, Next Big Thing will be forced to give up electricity, telephone communication and the wearing of anything that is not a plain, mid-calf-length dress. Oh yes, and she will have to wear a bonnet. You will too but what parent doesn't make sacrifices for their child?

ORANGE-OMETER

This book has already touched on the dangers of fake tan...

Oscar
(Golden)

Orange
(Orange)

Lindsay Lohan
(Beyond orange)

Tony Blair
(Unexpected)

Sun
(Fiery)

Jordan
(Ouch)

... but because it persists in being such a favourite of young starlets it is essential to drive the point home. If Next Big Thing creeps too high up the orange-ometer, stand her out on the patio and hose her down.

Reese's Pieces
(Delicious)

Donald Trump
(Wrong)

Halloween pumpkin
(Scary)

Sophie Anderton
(My eyes are burning)

Space hopper
(Menacing, yet bouncy)

Dale Winton
(Help! Help! Help! It's nuclear!)

THE NEXT BIG THING
On the Big Screen

It won't be long before Hollywood calls and you see the Next Big Thing herself in the cinema.

Meanwhile, here a few films she might enjoy:

10 Things I Hate About You	10 Things I Hate About Uniform
The Devil Wears Prada	The Daughter Wears Hand-Me-Downs, And Not Through Choice
Trainspotting	Trendspotting
The Sound of Music	The Sound of My Own Voice
Mean Girls	Me Me Me Girls
Girls Just Want To Have Fun	Girls Just Want To Have Fun At Your Expense
No Country For Old Men	No Country For Old And Unfashionable Parents
Casino Royale	Ego Royale
High School Musical	My School Musical, Starring Me
The Parent Trap	The Parents: Trapped
Groundhog Day	Grounded Again
I Am Legend	I Am Legend (Just You See)

KEIRA KNIGHTLEY

DAME JUDI DENCH

CREDIBLE NEXT BIG THING

NBT VENN: CREDIBLE NBT

Like Keira Knightley, Credible Next Big Thing is torn between wanting to be taken seriously as an actor – no smart-thinking thespian calls herself an 'actress' these days – and her innate need to pout in photographs. Credible Next Big Thing would like to have the gravitas of someone like Dame Judi Dench. Oh, and her Oscar. But seriously, does she have to be so old? Can't she wear something a little more revealing sometimes? Or at least stage a scandal in her personal life so she can cry prettily about press intrusion? It's tough out there.

LET MUSIC BE YOUR GUIDE
A song for every occasion!

When Next Big Thing is in a slump and needs a little jollying along from you, her esteemed mentor:

'You, you're such a big star to me
You're everything I wanna be
But you're stuck in a hole and I want you to get out
I don't know what there is to see
But I know it's time for you to leave
We're all just pushing along
Trying to figure it out, out, out'

Take That: 'Shine'

Has the Next Big Thing transformed you from geek to chic? Thank her with a few lines of this:

*'My friends said she's amazing and I
can't believe you got that girl
She gave me more street cred
I dug the book she read
How could I forget
She rocks my world
More than any other girl'*

McFly: 'That Girl'

If the fact it is raining isn't bad enough, Next Big Thing wants to hold the umbrella, despite the fact she is a foot or two shorter than you. Get her in line with this:

'Now that it's raining more than ever
Know that we still have each other
You can stand under MY umbrella
You can stand under MY umbrella
(Ella ella eh eh eh)
Under my umbrella
(ella ella eh eh eh)
Under my umbrella
(ella ella eh eh eh)
Under my umbrella
(ella ella eh eh eh eh eh eh)'

Rihanna: 'Umbrella'

If you make it through to the end of the 'eh's and 'ella's, Next Big Thing will probably be too embarrassed to stand next to you anyway. Result! The whole umbrella is yours.

Does Next Big Thing owe you some money? Hold your hands out Oliver Twist-style and sing your heart out with Britney Spears:

Gimme gimme more
Gimme (Uh)
Gimme gimme more
Gimme gimme more
Gimme more

Britney Spears: 'Gimme More'

Is 'Don't nag me!' a familiar refrain in your house, and one often directed at you? Silence Next Big Thing with one of her favourite songs:

'I'm not gonna stop
That's who I am
I'll give it all I got that is my
*   plan*
When I find what I lost
You know you can
Bet on it, bet on it, bet on it,
*   bet on it.'*

High School Musical 2: 'Bet On It'

49

THE ENTOURAGE

As a popular young lady,
Next Big Thing is
rarely alone.

Her ever present gaggle of girlfriends is a crucial element of her bid for celebrity; they are the people who support her when she is down and laugh at her jokes to make them seem even funnier.

When gathered together, Next Big Thing's entourage can be a little intimidating. They take over your home, leaving you to poke your head through your own door and timidly offer them a biscuit. Don't be fazed by the fact that they think you are patently uncool right now. That can change.

The hub of the friendship group is

Bebo, Facebook, myspace

or probably all three.

You will have noticed how Next Big Thing spends every spare hour sitting at her computer like a crack commander of special forces, chatting online. Set up your own profile, watch your popularity go up several pegs and marvel at the new intelligence you are gathering on Next Big Thing and her entourage.

First up is the crazy friend: the one even the teachers are scared of. However often she repeats her trademark line, 'God, I'm mental!' still the men in white coats do not take her away. She has wildly coloured hair and a voice that sounds like two hyenas struggling to make themselves heard in a packed nightclub. Her popularity is infectious, apparently, but you seem to have a natural inbuilt immunity.

Second: the boy-mad friend. She is either to be found delivering important messages like, 'My friend fancies your friend' or snogging behind the bike sheds. At all times, she has one or two boys on the go and is quite scarily possessive of them. It is possible you may one day find yourself in the position of getaway driver for the boy/s in question, just because you feel sorry for them.

The real worry is the rich friend, because she has everything Next Big Thing wants. Her clothes are all bang on-trend and her haircut cost more than your family holiday. Rich Girl is the reason Next Big Thing is never satisfied with the hand-me-downs you bestow upon her. It is possible Next Big Thing will spend as much time as possible at Rich Girl's house, hoping that her parents will take pity and adopt another daughter.

Everyone needs someone they can turn to in hours of need. Next Big Thing calls her quietest friend, who will listen for hours and is not familiar with the phrase, 'Get over yourself already.' She is a calming influence. Something about her reminds you of a bygone age when childhood was filled with hopscotch and innocent laughter, and teenagers as they are today simply did not exist. Welcome this girl into the bosom of your family and your life will be happier. Next Big Thing may feel somewhat jealous, but she will get over it by the time she is 21.

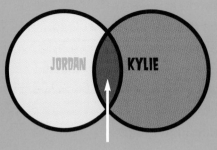

SHAMELESS NEXT BIG THING

NBT VENN: SHAMELESS NBT

You may mock Jordan for her lack of discernable talent and the peculiar shade of her skin, but she is a one-woman exercise in being rich and famous. Shameless Next Big Thing has studied Jordan's autobiographies as seriously as if they were post-nuclear attack survival guides. She would do well to take some tips from pint-size popette Kylie, who at least knocked out a 20-year career before she started doing lame brand extensions like a range of bedlinen. Shame on her. Shame on them all.

WHEN OPPORTUNITY KNOCKS...

The Next Big Thing is nothing short of remarkable, truly.

When faced with any difficult or potentially life-threatening situation, she has the incredible ability to turn it around with a single thought: 'Hey – this could be my big break!'

Say you get stuck in a crowded lift and everyone starts sweating and panicking the moment it becomes clear you really are trapped. For the Next Big Thing, this is an opportunity to raise the alarm with her breathtaking singing voice. The fire brigade will be with you faster than you can say, 'Give that girl her own show!'

LET'S TAKE THE FEAR FACTOR UP A NOTCH.

What goes through the Next Big Thing's head when your car crashes into the vehicle ahead on the motorway? No, not, 'Dad is a rubbish driver.' Instead: 'Everyone is slowing down to look at me!' The adrenaline kicks in, giving her superhuman strength to smash open the buckled car door and pull the whole family out to safety. As you lie dazed by the roadside, she takes your phone from your pocket to make an anonymous tip off to the national newspapers. Front page, here she comes.

All the story now requires is a love interest and a human tragedy. She wouldn't sacrifice you for the sake of a thrilling story, would she? Would she!

HOW TO
Embarrass The Next Big Thing

If she seriously wants to be famous, she needs toughening up. In the future she will be harassed by *heat* magazine's circle of shame, whereby her every bead of perspiration will be magnified and presented to the nation for their judgement. Yes, the world can be cruel and there are countless casualties along the path to fame. How can you prepare your darling Next Big Thing? Simple: give her a little dose of Shame Academy right now. She'll thank you later. Honest.

STAGE 1:

Offer to take her and a friend shopping then drop them off at the church jumble sale. Can she put a positive PR spin on that?

STAGE 2:

Pick her up from school on your bicycle and offer her a piggyback home. Does she accept with good grace?

STAGE 3:

Circulate family photos before she has a chance to airbrush them. Is she making plans to leave the country?

STAGE 4:

Accidentally wear the same outfit as her. But look nicer in it, obviously. Has she been swallowed up by the floor?

STAGE 5:

Convince all Next Big Thing's gullible friends that you used to be Madonna's body double. Does she blow your cover?

STAGE 6:

Quit wearing deodorant in an effort to spiritually reconnect with your own personal scent. Does she refuse to hold your hand in public, even in the fresh air?

STAGE 7:

Set up a Bebo profile and become online-friends with everyone in her class. Does she accuse you of 'damaging the brand'?

STAGE 8:

Throw a pair of old pants on your head and tell everyone you are related. Has she put a severed horse's head in your bed?

THE NEXT BIG THING
In Love

Any fool knows that if you want to be mega-mega-stratospherically famous, you need to get together with someone of similar potential.
A celebrity couple like David and Victoria Beckham are worth many more column inches together than they are apart. With that thought firmly in mind, the Next Big Thing is on the hunt.

When it comes to choosing a partner, it is common for the Next Big Thing to choose someone who is – how can we put this delicately? – a little out of her league. Like the beautiful, charismatic millionaire actor Johnny Depp, for instance. In the short-term, this is not such a bad thing; it pretty much guarantees Miss NBT will not be running off to Gretna Green before passing her GCSEs. However, long-term this unrealistic attitude to love can be the kind of issue that will cost her (read: YOU) thousands of pounds in therapy.

However, the Next Big Thing is no fool. Realising the logistical problems involved in an LA-based relationship, she picks a boy from her class at school to form a power couple with. So far, so mundane, so in order to grab a few headlines she needs some drama – the emotional equivalent of fire-eaters and lions, if you will. Their romance moves at quite a pace: first, she hates him. By the end of the week, he is her

soulmate and she is officially In Love. There are walks in the park with hand-holding, flowers, a glorious sunset and two-for-one McChicken sandwiches: all the key elements of modern romance.

But the good mood is shorter-lived than the unsettling mayonnaise-y McAftertaste. You see, then there follows a misunderstanding involving a text message and a third party. Mistrust causes tempers to fray and carefully manicured nails to be gnawed clean off. The relationship unravels noisily, with the whole school getting involved and taking sides. Brilliant. It is great to have everyone's attention. And what better way to keep it than to get back together with the Boy Who May Or May Not Have Done Her Wrong?

Having counselled her through the crisis, dealt out tissues and allowed her to swap regular nutrition-packed meals for emotionally comforting ice cream during the recovery period, you may wonder what the heck is going on. Well, get used to that feeling, because it is only going to intensify. The method in Next Big Thing's relationship madness only becomes clear when she brokers a million pound deal with *OK!* every time she and her boyfriend have a carefully staged spat.

MOTHER TERESA — PARIS HILTON

CHARITABLE NEXT BIG THING

NBT VENN: CHARITABLE NBT

God, if you're reading: sorry. But this has to be set straight: nobody wants to look like Mother Teresa. Sure, she was kind-hearted and she set a fine example of modern-day sainthood but young ladies everywhere cannot help but get freaked out by the explosion of wrinkles on her face. So, after a busy day drying tears down at the orphanage and helping lepers tie their shoelaces, Charitable Next Big Thing takes a leaf from Paris Hilton's book and gets herself a facialist on speed dial. Mother Teresa may have been ok without male admirers but not everyone is.

HAPPY BIRTHDAY,
Next Big Thing

'You don't need to get me a birthday present this year' is a phrase unlikely to ever pass Next Big Thing's lips. You need to start saving up for that gift six months in advance and allow a further six months to pay off your credit card bill, such is the cycle of life.

It is unlikely you will be short of ideas for what to get her, because she will be dropping hints like hot potatoes. However, trying to think of a present under the £200 mark might be a little tricky. (The list overleaf might help – now all you need to do is look on in pride as Next Big Thing tries to compose her best 'Is that for ME?' face.)

Next Big Thing's party is going to be massive, whether you like it or not. The countdown to her birthday involves a huge PR campaign, where her friends spread rumours of the party of the century throughout the school and her millions of Bebo friends. The first you hear of this is when the police warn you of the severe danger you are in.

In order to protect your home from an army of teenagers with E-numbers to burn, you must take control. Forget the mobile disco and the smoke machine:

ALL NEXT BIG THING REALLY WANTS IS A MAGICIAN WHO MAKES BALLOON ANIMALS.

That's real entertainment. Follow it up with a game of Sleeping Lions, where everyone has to lie as quiet and still as they possibly can. The winner receives a nice shiny apple.

Now, a birthday tea. Lentil salad will be particularly welcome, washed down with sugar-free lemonade. Play some nice relaxing Mozart to set the mood. Each child also gets a party bag to take home, with a copy of *Debrett's Etiquette* inside. Who wouldn't appreciate such a fine gift? Next Big Thing is already excited about next year's birthday.

PRESENT WISH-LIST*:

- a hand-knitted jumper,
  in the scratchiest wool you can find

- violin lessons,
  because nothing squawks 'star
  quality' quite like the violin

- a chess set,
  to keep up with the cool gang at
  school

- tickets
  to see the live studio final of
  Mastermind

- a paper bag
  to put over my head

*THE AUTHOR CANNOT ACCEPT RESPONSIBILITY FOR THE NEXT BIG THING'S
SATISFACTION WITH THESE GIFTS. YOU FOOL.

THE NEXT BIG THING
On Holiday

If a weekend break in the Caribbean is good enough for Kelly Brook, why can't you afford it too? Why? Why? Why? Why? Why?

For the Next Big Thing, seeing newspapers packed with pictures of celebrities **sucking their stomachs in on the beach is too much to bear.**

WHY MUST SHE BE STUCK IN GLOOMY OLD BRITAIN DURING THE WINTER MONTHS?

It can be hard to explain to her that it is normal for civilians to take only one holiday a year, and that cloudy half-term you spent on the Isle of Wight a few months ago is all she is getting.

In the good old days, it used to be that people went into travel agents to book holidays, which gave the whole process a certain gravitas and limited participation to adults only. Now, in our mega-speedy broadband age, you might discover that the Next Big Thing has started her own research into holiday destinations.

'What about Sandy Lane in Barbados?' she suggests, with an innocent brightness in her tone of voice, which will fast disappear when you point out that only mega-rich celebrities like Simon Cowell holiday there and it is not worth remortgaging your house in order to gain proximity to the mighty pop-puppeteer.

NEXT BIG THING'S PACKING ESSENTIALS:

- 21 of my favourite DVDs.
  Whaddya mean there's nothing to watch them on?

- 8 different pairs of shoes.
  (Dad will carry my suitcase)

- 9 sunglass options. Whoever said one
  pair would go with every outfit should be banished
  to BBC2

- Digital camera. and the means to upload
  photos onto the internet hour-by-hour so all my
  friends at home can see what an amazing holiday
  I'm having

- Tanning oil. so my skin can really sizzle – like
  pork scratchings

- Business cards. with my face and my agent's
  contact details, in the likely event I'll get spotted

Something closer to home, you suggest. She says: 'We could hire a yacht in the Med for the Cannes film festival?' Look interested, then pretend you are deep in thought and ignore the question.

Even when Next Big Thing has exhausted a range of hot holiday options, there is still the question of skiing to deal with. Though expensive, you relish the idea of separating her from her all-consuming grooming routine and getting her in touch with her inner child (last seen aged seven) as she plays on the slopes. Plus, there is a certain parental joy in wrapping her up safely in a helmet and padded trousers.

So, yes, a break in the mountains may be just what the child protection officer orders. Just take a few moments to prepare staff at the ski resort for the tantrum that is going to erupt when Next Big Thing discovers her package does not include Chanel carving skis like the ones modelled by Victoria Beckham.

As you might have guessed, the trick of successful holidaying with the Next Big Thing is to give the break a bit of celeb spin. For example, there is no way you will convince her to go camping on the Yorkshire Moors, but tell her your family has been selected to test a UK version of 'I'm A Celebrity, Get Me Out of Here' and she will be packing her wet-wipes faster than you can say, 'Action!' It is up to you whether you encourage Next Big Thing to go through with Moortucker trials and bite the head off that slug.

If nothing can persuade *you* to go camping and the idea of driving off to a hotel and leaving Next Big Thing next to the campfire alone seems rather heartless, there is another option.

You might not like it. Butlins.

Yes, it does raise pertinent questions of taste and style, but you can always be sure where the Next Big Thing is: on the stage. Her performance fee might even pay for your next holiday.

COMMUNICATION
Tips

Sometimes NBT seems so lost in her showbiz fantasies she can be hard to get through to. Do you even understand what she is going on about half the time? Does she know anything about the world on the other side of her sunglasses?

Try speaking her language to engage her in a deep and meaningful conversation:

'The eternal struggle between the diametrically opposed forces wrestling within the soul, breaking free of their physical prison and spiritually setting forth into the universe.'

OK, I'm going to work really hard at school, ace all my exams, take a year out to build a well in a remote Malawi village before going to work for the United Nations. Or an animal shelter in Dorset.'

'I've already started a conservation project where I pick up litter. My hands get very dirty and my soul gets clean.'

'You are so right! I am going to give up all my worldly possessions and dedicate the rest of my life to inner calm and charitable works.'

You are surprised – nay, floored – by the Next Big Thing's hidden depths. In fact, Next Big Thing's intellect and noble ambitions make you look rather bad by comparison. Now you feel inspired to contribute more to the greater good of the world yourself. Give yourself a hug.

'Omigod! OMG! It's you, isn't it?!'

Delivers withering look, channelled directly from Simon Cowell

repeat with even more enthusiasm

'What are you on about now?'

'If you mean your resident superstar, then yes!'

'Right here, girlfriend, right here! Hey, I was thinking today we could discuss the meaning of life. What's it all abaaaht?'

'It's been too long since we had a proper talk. I want to get to know the real you.'

'Can I go and watch TV now?'

'Getting a ginormous film contract / record deal / TV career as soon as possible that will earn me loads of money, make me hugely famous and cause every man to fall at my feet.'

'Moving out of home as soon as possible.'

'Oh dear, I'm not sure you will get the happy ending you dream of there. Maybe there's another way?'

'Why do you always have to ruin everything? You're just jealous because I'm prettier than you.'

'To be adopted by Angelina Jolie.'

'Mmm, interesting. Now, tell me, what would you like more than anything else in the world?'

'I think I might donate the television to a needy children's home and use all my new-found spare time to knit together the hole in the ozone layer.'

'An embarrassingly rich footballer-boyfriend to take me shopping.'

'World peace.'

'Yes it blinkin' is. Just give me £50 now and I'll show you.'

'Gosh, how admirable! How are you going to make that happen?'

'I don't think money is the answer to your problems.'

'I can't be bothered with the effort. I'd prefer to go shopping instead.'

'I'm going to teach the world to sing / In perfect harmony.'

Your best bet for a harmonious home is to take on a little of the Next Big Thing's joie de vivre yourself. Enter Miss Great Britain, shop yourself into bankruptcy, break into song when your boss is waving your P45 under your nose, and you too will be sequin-tastically happy.

THERE — DOESN'T BONDING FEEL GREAT?

WHAT'S GOING ON...

... inside The Next Big Thing's Head?

Is that Zac and Cody over there? Does my hair look OK?

Do I really have to thank my parents in my Oscar acceptance speech? How embarrassing.

I'm *click* ready *click* for *flash* my *flash* close-up *flash*.

Is my ego really so big it can be seen from space, or was Dad trying to wind me up again?

Does he fancy me? Join the queue, boy.

Who's that vision of gorgeousness in the mirror? Oh, it's me! Hel-*lo*...

Omigod, Mum *always* carries that handbag. Sack the stylist.

What will I wear to the Brit Awards?

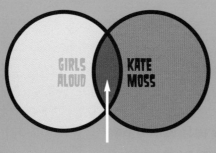

GIRLS ALOUD — KATE MOSS

FASHION-FORWARD NEXT BIG THING

NBT VENN: FASHION-FORWARD NBT

When you are part of a mega-successful pop band, the sad truth is you are not allowed to choose your own clothes, lest your outfit not match the other girls. Ok, so Girls Aloud mostly look like they're having fun, but there's always one of them who has to wear something a bit minging. So the answer is obvious: Fashion-forward Next Big Thing has to go a bit Kate Moss and choose her own fashion road. She is a lone wolf, always ahead of the Primark pack. And on the occassions she is photographed with friends, everyone can see she is the most beautiful. What an inspiring role model.

HOW TO COPE WITH THE NEXT BIG THING'S
Diva Fits

Whether it is insisting her lunchbox be packed to a certain symmetry or her Nesquik is only ever stirred anti-clockwise, the Next Big Thing has turned getting her own way into a fine art.

But what about when she doesn't? The diva strop when that happens can be impressive…

'I promise I will make you breakfast in bed'

It is difficult to stay firm when you are faced with wet-eyed pleading and straightforward bribery. But can you really trust Next Big Thing to cook your eggs just how you like them? Imagine their rubbery texture balancing delicately in your stomach and your willpower will harden.

'What do you mean, "No"?'

Oh dear. Now you've gone and done it. Look at her: right now Next Big Thing is blinking in confusion, trying to register how on earth it might have come about that she is not getting what she wants. Do you know what you're getting yourself into? Can't you just fold now? No?

'I can't believe you are trying to hurt me like this!'
You feel inclined to remind her that giving birth to her was so painful you actually bit through a wooden cheese board. There is pain on both sides. You get over it. In years to come, you will hug each other and laugh about this silly falling-out. Now, however, she is shaking her darling little fist at you.

'I hate you! I hate you! I HATE YOU!'
You are bearing witness to a full-blown foot-stamping tantrum. And now tears are falling too. Pretty ones, naturally, but it is hard to watch just the same. Give in now, and you could escape without permanent psychological damage but you will forever feel totally 'played'. Be strong – don't give in now when you are a mere sniff away from the finish line. Tell Next Big Thing she can write this fight up in her autobiography and her fans will love her all the more for it. Every great artist suffers.

'Why are you being so unfair?'
Now is the time to double-check whether it is worth making a stand against letting Next Big Thing go to an all-night party with people of the opposite sex, possibly the entire stock of Threshers and definitely no parental supervision. And are you really tough enough to see this fight through?

THE NEXT BIG THING
In the Future

If The Next Big Thing doesn't get a number one album, an Oscar or a kiss from Jason Orange, all is not lost.

Her showbiz skills can still be put to good use at

30

in one of these possible careers...

FOOTBALLER

Finally, Next Big Thing realises the smart money is made on the pitch instead of tracking the players down on the town. The only thorn in her side is the fact the rest of her team insist on wearing exactly the same outfit as her – how is her star potential supposed to shine?

FARMER

After hearing so many celebrities reveal to magazines how much they want to run away from the fame circus and live in the country, Next Big Thing throws her belongings into a horse trailer and settles in the wilds of Yorkshire. 'It *is* glamorous' she says through gritted teeth as she mucks out the pigsty every day.

PRIME MINISTER

Politicians get a bad press. A politician who can entertain the nation and lend a palpable air of excitement to tedious debates in the House of Commons is going to get votes aplenty.

TEACHER

'Honestly, there is no point wasting time learning long division – I haven't used it since I was 11,' she says, and children flourish under her wise words.

SPEED CAMERA-CHECKER

The Next Big Thing is so keen on having her photograph taken, she is prepared to drive her car over the speed limit to check the speed cameras are snapping the right people.

BARRISTER

Not only does she get to dress up
every time she goes to work, she
actually has someone's whole future
depend on how well she performs.
If that's not an incentive to give the
show of your life, what is?

ADVERTISING EXECUTIVE

All those years spent convincing you that she needs a puppy /
earmuffs / a diamante encrusted yacht are valuable training
for persuading other people to buy things they will never,
ever need.

COULD I BE THE NEXT BIG THING?

Fame isn't so scary now, is it?

In fact, having read all this research you probably want a taste of the celebrity action yourself. All it takes is stubborn belief in your innate, unspecified talents and – *ta da!* – fame and fortune are yours. Take a moment to stand back and soak up the applause. They're cheering for you! YOU!